## Praise for *Stop Hiring Failures!* from business experts:

Wow – what a great book! You must be a magician to have packed so much information into such a compact package. Every paragraph contains at least one practical tip. Your checklist will be invaluable for future interviews. You said I would be "shocked" when thinking of past interviews. Guilty as charged. I was shocked as I recognized my numerous interviewing errors.

"I told way too many stories and regularly divulged my job requirements. No wonder candidates always gave me the "right" answers. I love your writing style, short and to the point. No fluff or boring stories to prove how clever you are, just lots of easy- to- follow information presented in a logical sequence. Whether you're a novice conducting your first interview or a seasoned veteran like me, everyone will benefit from this informative book."
– *Karen L. Schippers, Chief Financial Officer, Welty Building Company LTD.*

"As a former CEO with Pulte Homes, Inc., a Fortune 200 company, and now actively involved with small companies through the private equity industry, I found Steve Springer's approach to the recruiting process to be both educational and thought-provoking. Over the years, I and my coworkers have experienced the pain and expense of bad hiring decisions. Unfortunately, most of these decisions were our fault because we didn't spend the time understanding the attributes that would make an individual successful with our company.

"Had we followed Steve's simple and straightforward approach to matching the right individual to the position within the organization, our success rate would have been dramatically improved. I highly recommend this outstanding book to all who want to improve their

process for hiring the best people for their companies, regardless of the size of the organization or the level of the position."
– *Robert K. Burgess, Former CEO, Pulte Homes*

"The sixty minutes it takes to read *Stop Hiring Failures!* just might be the best business investment decision hiring managers could make. As an Executive Recruiter for the past twenty-five years, I have been responsible for hundreds of senior level search assignments for large corporations and smaller entrepreneurial organizations. Few of these search engagements came to us a part of a strategic growth plan, but rather as an urgent need for someone to fill a position "yesterday."

"Many of these urgent needs were sudden replacements for individuals hired within the last year. These people left their jobs, or were let go, because of confused or poorly defined expectations. The steps put forth in Steve Springer's book will help growing organizations avoid crisis hires and resulting failures."
– *Linda Patrick Madden, Principal, Madden Associates*

"Having spent most of my career in a variety of Senior Human Resource positions at large companies like Frito Lay, Pepsi Cola and Pulte Homes, I have probably interviewed and hired thousands of people at all levels in an organization. I have had mostly successes but also a few failures. More recently I have been faced with the same challenging task at several smaller companies that I'm involved with, where the consequences of making even one bad hiring decision are enormous.

"Steve's book has very artfully and practically captured many of the key principles and techniques that a professional hiring manager often takes years to develop. He explains them in a manner that will enable the untrained manager to minimize and possibly eliminate the very common and often fatal "hiring mistakes."

"Think of this book as a very inexpensive insurance policy that pays off big when the stakes are high. Steve also makes his book very enjoyable to read by illustrating some of his key points with very interesting and oftentimes humorous analogies. Remember, no one ever hires the perfect person (they don't exist), but this is one time that getting close really matters."
– *Michael A. O'Brien, Managing Partner, Croston Partners*

"There have been a lot of good business books, but I can't recall one that, in sixty to ninety minutes, gives the reader step-by-step instruction on how to avoid one of the most expensive mistakes in business. Your book does just that by preventing a bad key-person hire. Many readers will put it to use immediately. Talk about value!

"I've been around the hiring process of thousands of key people over the past thirty years, advising the job-seeker rather than the employer. I can assure you, if readers follow your advice, they will consistently hire key people who fit well in their culture and meet or exceed all expectations. Everyone knows how much a bad hire at these levels costs. Wasted time and money are the least of it. The real cost? Losing momentum, getting off track, not achieving vital milestones, lagging behind competitors – because you selected the wrong person to lead your efforts in a function critical to success.

"Most business owners, executives and managers have made a bad hire at least once. Happily, if they follow the steps in your book, it will never happen to them again. When your book gets out there, as it should, people on both sides will be in your debt. Just as no one wants to make a bad hire, neither does anyone want to get hired into an organization where they don't fit."
– *Dan McAneny, Dan McAneny Associates*

# Stop Hiring Failures!

Steve Springer

ISBN : 1-4196-4705-9


To order additional copies, please contact us.
BookSurge, LLC
www.booksurge.com
1-866-308-6235
orders@booksurge.com

# Stop Hiring Failures!

*This book is dedicated to my wife Carol, my lover, best friend and soul mate.*

# Table of Contents

# INTRODUCTION

## Why Have You Hired Failures in the Past?

Why has your hiring process failed you? You're devastated. And confused. You hired a superbly qualified senior manager seven months ago and yesterday she gave her two weeks' notice. She felt her management style was incompatible with that of the other managers. A quick replacement is vital to the success of a major project.

Five weeks ago you fired a technical manager you had hired just ten months ago. He had world-class credentials, including an advanced degree from a top school. But he had the energy level of a snail and his leadership skills were nonexistent.

To replace him, you contacted a recruiter and, miraculously, she sourced an outstanding candidate. That interview is scheduled for this morning, but you've been buried and have yet to review the resume. You had hoped to read it first thing, but your early arrival at the office was quickly interrupted by a subordinate whose crisis demanded your immediate attention. Your assistant just announced that the candidate has arrived, so you desperately dig through your pile of papers, retrieve the resume, and quickly scan it to make sure you at least get the name right. Sound familiar?

Why did you fail to select the right candidate last time? How should you interview this person to ensure you don't repeat your past errors? How do you predict who will succeed in your organization?

## Why the Process Fails

Unfortunately, most managers and executives never invest the time required to hire the best candidate. Most spend more time planning a company party or sales banquet than they spend on recruiting top talent. But what could be more vital to your business success than hiring outstanding people?

Your poor selection track record is not unique. Just look at the *Wall Street Journal* or nightly business news for proof. Top executives often fail after short tenures, even at corporate giants. And consider your own business. How many employees have quit or been fired after less than a year of service?

It might surprise you, but you could have uncovered who was likely to fail during the interviewing process. In most cases, your turnover was not caused by a lack of technical expertise or education, but by a poor cultural fit or inappropriate management style. So how do you spot these fatal flaws?

## I Don't Have the Time!

I see you scowling, wrinkle lines deeply etching your face, because you just don't have the time to rethink your selection process – and no one on your staff does, either. However, you will spend countless hours analyzing and evaluating a significant equipment purchase or capital expenditure before making the final decision. But spend an equal amount of time when making a hiring decision? – *Impossible*!

Ask yourself: *What will impact my business **more** than attracting and retaining top talent?*

It is never merely equipment or other capital expenditures that make your business work. These simply provide the tools that assist your employees in accomplishing goals, completing projects, developing new products and solving customer problems that will move your organization in the desired direction.

Nothing impacts your business more than hiring quality people. And improving your employee selection process can be fun! It will help you reassess your organization, your culture and your goals. It will enable your top decision-makers to precisely identify the type of person who thrives in your environment. It will also create information about your company that can be applied to the selection of employees at all levels. It will ultimately increase the effectiveness of your entire team, especially your new hires.

The process is logical and straightforward. The steps include:
- gathering information to understand your unique requirements
- searching inside your organization for hidden talent
- preparing for and conducting an effective interview that will surprise and delight you with the information you uncover
- evaluating candidates
- conducting that important second interview
- checking backgrounds
- making the offer

This book covers a vast amount of information in a condensed form. To allow you to read without taking copious notes, Appendix B contains a checklist of each step, in the order presented in the book.

As you learn this selection process, some suggestions may seem familiar. However, many concepts will be new. The process will reveal glaring flaws in your current interviewing approach that will shock you. If you conduct only one interview following the recommended steps, you will experience the incredible power of this approach. So let's begin this adventure!

# STEP ONE

# ESTABLISH YOUR SELECTION CRITERIA

### First – Determine Your Requirements

A sound employee selection outcome starts with an information gathering process. As you analyze your business and identify job requirements, record your thoughts so that you can later share them with others on your team. This information will help guide you and your team as you create your selection criteria.

To infuse your business with outstanding talent, you must define the key factors essential for success in your organization. First, analyze your business. List your key products or services, plus any planned offerings. Next, describe *in detail* the role of the new hire in all of these areas of your business. List all of those he will interact with, both inside and outside your organization, and the nature of these interactions. Include critical problems that need resolution, crucial projects that must be completed, and pivotal relationships that must be created or improved.

Review the job description, if one exists, and list the technical skills, knowledge and education required. Include any licensing requirements, certifications or similar prerequisites. Next, create an inventory of the major duties and tasks of the position. Then, list the type and level of prior work experience required to assume these duties. Finally, create a list of peers, subordinates or other individuals who possess intimate knowledge of these qualifications and request their input. Their knowledge is often superior to yours in some areas, and they will invariably redefine the job to include essential factors that you have overlooked.

Believe it or not, that was the easy part; the part a few managers do reasonably well. Analyzing your business and the education and technical requirements of the position are relatively straightforward. The more difficult but essential task: defining the type of person who will excel in your organization.

You and your staff are probably the least qualified to make this assessment. The longer you have worked for an organization, the less able you are to objectively define your culture. Remember: *fish discover water last*. Insiders rarely have an objective view of the idiosyncrasies of their culture or business. To gain the required perspective, find an external advisor who will ask the tough questions, interview key employees and create an accurate, objective assessment of your work environment, values, style and culture.

This advisor could be a trusted executive recruiter with whom you have a long relationship. The advisor might be an attorney, lender or investor who has the required skills. You might choose a vendor or supplier who has a vested interest in your success. As you continue reading, think about the skills and objectivity required for this vital external advisor role, then consider those you know who could perform this important function.

**Understand Your Unique Culture**

Do you state that your company encourages risk, but your staff knows that 100 percent success is always required? Do you proudly boast that your employees are your most important asset, but your pay levels are below par? Does your mission statement declare that the customer always comes first, but your staff knows that customers come after profits? It is unlikely that your employees will confront you with these inconsistencies.

To gain an honest appraisal of your true beliefs, unique style, values and approach to business, recruit an outside advisor. An external advisor should meet with you, your direct reports and at least one other level of management to gain insight into how things are done in your culture. During these private meetings, in which confidentiality must be guaranteed, this consultant should ask your managers to explain their reasons for joining your organization, their most positive experiences and their biggest disappointments.

The questions should explore such areas as management style and practices, customer relations, attitudes toward quality, willingness of management to involve employees in decision-making, etc. If some of these individuals have direct knowledge of the duties, tasks or projects of the position to be filled, they should be asked to share their perspective regarding those job requirements.

Someone outside of your organization will pose the questions that no insider would consider. Someone with no knowledge of your industry will challenge conventional wisdom on how things "must be done" in your business. This advisor will accurately identify, in a way you cannot, all the key factors required to thrive in your organization.

When creating a list of the critical job criteria that predict success, this advisor must understand the various relationships that a new hire will have with those outside your organization, including customers, suppliers, vendors or government agencies. What is the nature of each of these relationships? In looking at past interactions, what approaches have proven successful and which have failed?

For example, assume that the position for which you are recruiting requires extensive negotiation skills with international suppliers. If the meetings occur in some areas of the Middle East, a successful negotiator will forcefully shout, punctuating his ultimatums with vigorous hand gestures, then storm out of the meeting after threatening to terminate the business relationship. In that area of the world, this approach earns respect. In Japan, one might experience a different reaction. So, who must your new hire interact with outside your organization, and what style or approach has proven to be most effective?

As part of the information gathering process, your external advisor should also interview non-management employees. Since employees are often reluctant to provide negative information to management, an outsider will generally obtain a more candid response. An effective advisor will ask each person to describe the nature of internal relationships, especially his or her relationship with the open position.

This external consultant will encourage these individuals to share their perceptions of those who have held this open position in the past, describing the behaviors that were most and least effective. These non-management employees should also be asked to share any knowledge of the technical requirements of the position. At the completion of these interviews, the advisor will have a comprehensive list of the skills and characteristics essential for success, as well as those that have resulted in failure.

If possible, the information gathering process should include interviews with key outside resources, including customers, suppliers, vendors and government agencies. Discuss their needs and their perceptions regarding the characteristics of the ideal potential candidate. Ask about past relationships with those who have held the position and what made those interactions positive or negative.

At the conclusion of all of these internal and external interviews, your external advisor should summarize his or her findings in a written report. You may be shocked by what you read.

## Decide on the Critical Success Criteria

*The profile of a successful new hire is now emerging.* Invite three to five managers and/or staff members to a meeting to share what you have learned and discuss the requirements for selecting a successful replacement. If you have recruited an outside advisor, ask him to facilitate the meeting. Since your external consultant has interviewed a number of your employees, he will possess unique insights regarding your culture and can challenge your thinking throughout the job-defining process.

Using a flip chart, start by listing the skills, abilities, knowledge, education, certification and so on that are absolutely essential for success. Focus on the day-to-day tasks and duties that must be managed or completed. Exclude items that could be quickly learned on the job or could be, at least temporarily, performed by someone else.

Next, list the prior work experience that is required for the open position. Discuss the specific type of tasks, duties and responsibilities an applicant must have had. This could include technical issues, number and/or level of people supervised, budget size, decision authority, scope of projects or other factors that would indicate that an individual has performed at or near the level that the open position requires.

Next, list the important projects that must be completed, the critical problems that must be tackled, the relationships that must be enhanced, the government agencies that require special attention and anything else that the candidate must effectively deal with during the first twelve months on the job. Be specific in terms of time deadlines, dollars involved or other factors. Describe how success will be measured or evaluated for each item listed. Create a second list for challenges that must be overcome in the next one to two years, including the measures of a successful outcome.

When assessing the open position, record any special requirements such as: the frequency and duration of domestic or foreign travel, the requirement to oversee a 24/7 operation, the need to relocate often, regular weekend meetings or other factors that might be required. Although you may consider these as normal or routine, someone outside your culture may be unwilling to commit to these job demands. Be especially sensitive to items of this type that caused turnover in the past.

Consider your culture. List words or phrases that describe your business philosophies, approach to customers or attitude regarding quality. Make this a fun task that involves everyone and record *every* suggestion – serious or funny, positive or negative. "Where the weak are killed and eaten" or "Profits first, profits last, profits always" may not be added to your corporate logo, but they may be an honest statement about your culture. When you have finished creating your list, decide on the top four or five words or phrases that best typify your organization's philosophies.

Next, list the personality characteristics, style, work ethic and values that a potential new hire must possess to fit into your work environment. Use words or phrases that exemplify your approach to customers, relationship with suppliers or outside agencies, dedication to quality, attitude toward employees, focus on innovation, commitment to the bottom line, or other meaningful descriptors. Again, solicit suggestions from everyone and record every idea, no matter how ridiculous it may seem. After you have collected ten to twenty responses, select the top four to six that are essential for your work environment.

By now, you have collected the vital information you will need to select the best candidate for the position. Next, you will use this information to create a list of the Critical Success Criteria that will guide the selection process.

Return to the information you recorded during this meeting. First, select the most critical four or five skills, abilities, knowledge, education, etc., required for this position. Next, list the specific prior work experience that is essential. Review the critical projects list you created, then decide on the most important three to five types of work experience a candidate *must* have had.

Discuss your culture and work environment, then list the three to five personality characteristics, management styles, values and so on that a potential candidate must possess to succeed in your organization. Since most selection failures are due to a poor fit between your culture and the values, style or personality of new hires, spend additional time on this section to ensure that you have clearly defined your requirements. Finally, add any unique work issues, such as travel or unusual work hours, to your list.

## Agree on the Priorities and Meaning

Post the Critical Success Criteria you have developed for everyone to review. Discuss why these are essential, and delete any items that the group feels are simply preferred rather than required. When you have finished, select the crucial six to nine items *in priority order*. **These Critical Success Criteria will be the focus of your screening and selection process.** Although all of the remaining items are important, it is nearly impossible to conduct an effective interview while trying to concentrate on ten to twenty or more diverse factors.

Discuss each of the six to nine items to ensure that there is a consensus regarding the meaning of each. Ask the group to provide examples of specific behaviors that a potential candidate might mention which would be indicative of a specific criteria. For example, if you list includes "win-win supplier relations," a candidate might boast of how he repaired a poor relationship with a supplier or worked with a supplier to resolve a problem while considering the supplicr's needs, or how a price change was negotiated with a supplier that both parties felt was fair.

*It is vital that those involved in the selection process are in agreement on the meaning of each of the Critical Success Criteria.* If necessary, rewrite the list, substituting terms or phrases that better describe the needs of your organization. Although time-consuming, this discussion process will ensure that there is alignment among your team on the factors that will result in recruiting a superior candidate.

# STEP TWO

# START YOUR SEARCH

## First – Look Inside

Before engaging a recruiter or advertising your opening, look inside your organization for potential candidates. Using the Critical Success Criteria, evaluate each person in relation to those criteria. It is unlikely that anyone is a perfect match but it is also unlikely that you will find an ideal candidate outside your company. Outside recruits always emphasize their strengths, talents and successes, but generally fail to divulge their shortcomings, idiosyncrasies or failures. With insiders, you know their limitations.

Any current employees who are even close to matching your criteria should be interviewed for the position. These interviews provide several benefits. First, employees will appreciate that they were viewed as possible candidates for the position. This will minimize any tendency for them to quit, frustrated that they were never even considered for this job opportunity.

Second, employees are more likely to cooperate with a new hire if they have had the opportunity to apply for the open position. If you determine that an employee is not currently qualified, provide specific feedback on the steps required to be considered for similar openings in the future. This information should assure rejected employees of your commitment to their career growth.

Third, these interviews will provide you and the others involved in the selection process the opportunity to hone and perfect your interviewing skills. When interviewing internal candidates, use the same process described in STEP FOUR – CONDUCT THE INTERVIEW.

Finally, and often surprisingly, one of your current employees might actually be the best choice for the position. By focusing on the Critical Success Criteria rather than subjective opinions, you might discover a talented individual you otherwise would have overlooked.

## Start the External Search

Now that you have developed a clear picture of the requirements for the position and eliminated any internal candidates, start your recruiting process. You may want to place job advertisements in newspapers or trade publications based upon your Critical Success Criteria. Consider contacting business associates or employees who may be able to refer a possible candidate.

You may prefer to contact an executive recruiter. If so, share the information you have gathered and the priorities you have established. A competent recruiter will ask a series of questions to clarify your needs and ensure agreement on the Critical Success Criteria. The recruiter should discuss with you the industries or professions that would most likely yield a successful candidate. Ideally, a recruiter will suggest other industries or professions that you never would have considered. This is the advantage of focusing on the criteria, not the job title. You will cast a wider net in your selection process, since you have focused on the outcomes and behaviors required, not the job title.

## Select the Interviewers

Before any resumes arrive, select the two to four individuals who will participate with you in the interviewing process. You might include people with strong technical knowledge, peers, investors or even subordinates who have the ability to objectively evaluate a potential boss. If you really want to think outside the box, consider asking a major customer, vendor or supplier to assist you with the selection process. If you have retained an outside advisor, definitely include him or her.

Meet as a group to agree on the role of each person in the interviewing process. Since each person will be conducting a one-on-one interview with each candidate, some interviewers may wish to concentrate their questions on the Critical Success Criteria they understand best. For example, one of the interviewers may volunteer to focus on the technical aspects of the position; another may be more qualified to evaluate management skills; and someone else may be better suited to evaluate an applicant's financial knowledge.

# STEP THREE

# PREPARE FOR THE INTERVIEW

## Interview Preparation Is Essential

*T*he Critical Success Criteria are the basis for conducting the interview. Even though some interviewers may feel qualified in only one aspect of the job, every interviewer should attempt to evaluate each candidate on every one of the Critical Success Criteria, not just the ones within his or her area of expertise. Most untrained interviewers will be surprised at their ability to critically evaluate a candidate on every aspect of the position and support that evaluation with objective information gained during the interview.

The interviewers must prepare for the interview. Although each person may take a somewhat different approach in conducting the interview, the process requires structure to be effective. *An effective interview is not a casual conversation or an unstructured discussion.* Allowing the applicant to take control of the interview process will guarantee that important information, especially facts detrimental to the interviewee, will be missed. Unfortunately, most interviewers have spent years conducting interviews in this fashion and rarely have taken the time to adequately prepare.

The best interviews start with a plan. In terms of the sequence of the interview, asking questions in a chronological order generally works best. Starting with education, you need to understand the candidate's course of learning and the reason for choosing that field of study. This sequence also allows you to evaluate the person's career in a logical order.

You want to explore each position held to see if there has been a progressive increase in responsibility, number of people supervised, budget authority, etc. If not, it should prompt you to ask follow-up questions to understand why. Keeping the interview in chronological order will also reveal any gaps in employment. Such gaps may have a logical explanation, or they may reveal an involuntary termination, which is generally an important piece of information.

Prior to the interview, review the Critical Success Criteria and the applicant's resume, and write down any specific questions that seem relevant. Also note any inconsistencies, such as titles not consistent with apparent duties, gaps between jobs, short tenure in a series of positions or other items of concern. Although all interviews share a common approach, each interview will be unique due to the varied background of each candidate.

# STEP FOUR

# CONDUCT THE INTERVIEW

## Interview Basics

Clear your schedule to ensure adequate time for the interview. The time required will vary depending upon the level of the position, the amount of the interviewee's relevant experience and the personality of the applicant. Budget at least two hours so that you don't rush the process.

If possible, conduct the interview in a conference room or similar site. Your office contains numerous distractions: the incessantly ringing phone, a pulsing computer screen or an overflowing in-box. Even your desk creates a psychological barrier, asserting your superior position. You want to make every effort to relax the applicant and encourage the free flow of information, both positive and negative. A more neutral meeting site will facilitate that process.

Your culture may encourage unplanned interruptions from peers or subordinates demanding an immediate answer to a pressing question. A closed office door may not provide a sufficient deterrent. If necessary, conduct the interview off-site, but never in a restaurant. Talk about interruptions! Eating and interviewing don't mix.

After greeting the applicant and offering a beverage, if available, take control of the interview by outlining the interview process. Describe the sequence you will follow: first, a discussion of education or training related to the position; next, a discussion of the candidate's career, starting with the first relevant position; finally, a discussion of the applicant's career goals and direction. Since several interviewers will be talking with each applicant, explain that the final interviewer of the day will discuss the position and company, and will answer any questions that the applicant may have.

You want to avoid providing the candidate with any information that reveals your requirements for the position prior to the last interview. Why? Because most applicants will attempt to present their background in the best possible light in terms of your needs. If you indicate, for example, that a comprehensive understanding of finance is essential, most applicants will emphasize this part of their skill set, even if they need to stretch the truth. *Never reveal your Critical Success Criteria during the interview process.*

## Getting the Interview Started

Ask the applicant to start by describing his education or training, especially as it relates to the position. Next, ask the applicant to discuss the first job or position that is relevant to your opening. Sometimes this will be the first position listed on the resume, but often it is a position that was omitted. Let the applicant decide on the best place to start. For each position held, ask the interviewee to explain the reason for accepting a position with that organization.

As he explains that first position, encourage him to describe the tasks or duties in detail. Attempt to gain an understanding of the level of responsibilities, number of people supervised, budget size or other relevant information. Probe to uncover what was accomplished, projects completed, sales gained or other facts related to the job criteria. Also, ask about disappointments or results that fell below expectations.

Explore relationships with peers, subordinates and superiors and the nature of those relationships. Ask the applicant to describe one successful outcome in detail, including his role in achieving that positive outcome. Uncover what he liked most about a specific position, any aspects that were disliked, and what led him to leave the organization or move to another position within that company.

As the applicant describes his relationship with a former supervisor, ask for a phone number for that person. If he doesn't recall a phone number, ask him to provide it after the interview, even if that person has left the organization. A home phone number will do. Attempt to collect the phone numbers of at least two or three prior supervisors.

Make it clear that you intend to call several prior bosses as part of your background investigation. Armed with the knowledge that you actually intend to talk with these individuals, applicants are remarkably accurate in describing job duties, levels of responsibility, accomplishments and even the failures they suffered.

Ask the applicant about relations with others. Asking how *others* would describe the applicant is a surprisingly successful approach. For example, ask: "If I brought all of your subordinates together, how would they describe your management style? What would they say they liked most about you, or least? How would they say you could most improve your management skills?"

When interviewees are asked this series of questions in this manner, they often provide a refreshingly honest appraisal of their management strengths and weaknesses. You will often see applicants pause and look up as they imagine this assembly of former employees providing this feedback. Frequently, candidates will then provide a surprisingly candid and critical assessment of their management style. You rarely get this level of candor if you simply ask applicants to describe *their* assessment of their management style. (Appendix A contains additional questions you could ask during the interview process.)

Continue the interview in a chronological order. Feel free to repeat questions about responsibilities, relationships, accomplishments and so forth. If you find certain questions yield thoughtful, comprehensive answers, by all means employ them as often as possible. Since each answer will be different, the applicant won't even notice the repetition.

## There Are No Wrong Answers!

It is crucial to remember that *there are no wrong answers* to your questions. There are only honest answers. If an applicant reveals that he dislikes performing a task that you feel is critical, that is not a wrong answer or a bad answer. It is the right answer, expressing the candidate's sincere attitude regarding this task. As an interviewer, your main goal is to obtain sincere responses as they relate to the Critical Success Criteria.

Never tell a candidate that his answer is inconsistent with your needs. Never reveal to an applicant your Critical Success Criteria. Never reveal how a response compares – positively or negatively – to your selection criteria. Avoid body language or nonverbal cues that will alert the applicant that the answer given was incompatible with your needs. If you provide *any* negative feedback, most candidates will quickly reverse their responses in an attempt to meet the requirements of the position.

Regardless of the information provided by the interviewee, always offer a positive response by smiling, nodding or otherwise showing agreement. Your job as the interviewer is to obtain as much information as possible, including any evidence that indicates a poor match to your requirements.

## Listening Is More Than Hearing

*Don't confuse hearing with listening.* Hearing is when your child describes a school assembly or your husband recounts a magnificent golf game. You listen enough to show interest while your mind is occupied with other matters. If you want to extract the maximum value from an interview, you need to focus 100 percent of your attention on the interviewee and not let your mind drift to other issues. That is easier said than done.

If you can't conduct the interview in a conference room, at least minimize distractions by moving away from your desk. That overwhelming to-do list and paper-strewn desk are guaranteed to redirect your thinking elsewhere. As the applicant talks, maintain eye contact as much as possible while you record brief notes of the discussion. To encourage the candidate to continuing talking, provide positive feedback by nodding, smiling, saying "uh huh" or giving similar responses. Avoid being put-off by accents or slower than normal speech patterns.

If the interviewee relates an experience similar to one that you have had, resist the urge to tell your story. *You learn nothing when you are talking*. In fact, this is the most common error committed by poor interviewers – talking rather than listening. Yes, we all take pleasure in the sound of our own sweet voice, and we all have a favorite story we love to tell. And during the interview, the applicant is guaranteed to be an attentive, enthusiastic listener; what other choice does he have?

In fact, *the most accurate measure of an effective interview is to compare how much you talked rather than listened.* Other than asking questions or paraphrasing the response of the interviewee, you should have talked very little. How does that measure of effectiveness compare to the interviews you have conducted in the past?

As the candidate talks, summarize his responses in your mind. Constantly compare his answers to your Critical Success Criteria. If you are uncertain as to the meaning of a response, ask a follow-up question to clarify the issue. Attempt to uncover several examples from the applicant's past that are directly related to each Critical Success Criteria, either positively or negatively.

Periodically, provide feedback by paraphrasing what you have learned. This will assure the applicant that you have been actively listening, and will force you to focus on both their words and the underlying meaning. By summarizing your understanding, you reassure the candidate that an accurate exchange of information has occurred.

*Pay attention to what is not said.* This includes any visual clues that indicate the candidate is uncomfortable with the topic, such as fidgeting, flushed skin or changes in posture. Any such response should trigger you to probe this topic in more detail.

Also, watch for any efforts to avoid an answer through incomplete responses, a lack of detail or anything else that might be inconsistent with an expected response. When in doubt, probe for more information. Keep probing until you are satisfied that you have received a complete, accurate answer to your question.

## Ask the Tough Questions Then SHUT UP!

If an applicant has read my bestseller, *How to Take Control of the Interview and Get the Job, Even if You Aren't Remotely Qualified,* he will easily avoid any tough questions you may ask. Most interviewers hate silence. If they ask a question and the applicant doesn't respond within a nanosecond, they will either rephrase the question to make it easier, ask a different question or, worst of all, answer their own question. *Silence is your friend.*

If you pose a potent probing question, the interviewee *should* need to pause and think about the answer. Often, a difficult question will cause applicants to look away as they struggle to form a response. That is what you want! Cogent questions cause candidates to pause and ponder their answers as they recall past challenges, problems or issues and their role in resolving them.

Also, more introverted or introspective candidates require a two-part process when asked a question. First, they hear your question. Next, they need to ask themselves that question inside their mind. These applicants may silently ponder their response for ten to twenty seconds, an eternity for many interviewers. If you simply smile and wait, these internally focused individuals will often provide an in-depth response of incredible complexity and detail.

If you ask a question and the applicant asks for clarification, simply provide that additional information and wait for a response. Learn to patiently wait for an answer rather than jumping in to fill the quiet void. You will be pleasantly rewarded.

## Probing Questions Maintain the Flow

Most interviewers will write a short list of questions in advance of the interview to make sure that they cover specific facts or issues. Often, after reading a resume, one or more questions will be suggested for that applicant. However, it is not necessary to create pages of questions.

*Keep the Critical Success Criteria list in front of you during the interview.* It will provide a constant reminder of the key issues that you must address during the interview. Also, decide in advance on the sequence you plan to follow, usually a chronological review of the applicant's career. Once you have explained the order of the interview, most applicants will find it easy to tell their career story, with minimal prompting.

As the applicant responds to your questions, employ probing follow-up questions to encourage the interviewee to provide more detail on an area of interest. For example, if an applicant has mentioned an important fact, indicate your desire for more information by a probing question such as: Why did that happen? What was your role in that? What was the result of your action? These probing follow-up responses encourage the candidate to provide more information on that topic.

One of the simplest but most effective probes is, "Oh?" This one-word response immediately telegraphs your need for more information and keeps the candidate talking.

Other probes could include: Could you be more specific? Please give me an example. Why do you think that happened? How did your customer react? How would you do it differently next time? To ensure that you have a complete picture, ask follow-up questions about the number of people involved, dollars, percentages, timelines or other relevant facts. Probe to make certain you understand the applicant's role and level of responsibility in accomplishing a task, executing a project or managing a budget. (Look in Appendix A for more examples of probing questions.)

There is one more powerful probe to consider. If the applicant's response is incomplete and you want more information, say nothing when he appears to have completed his answer. Silence is a powerful communicator that often compels a more complete response. Although over-use of silence may cause some applicants distress, it is a simple, effective way to encourage the interviewee to provide more information.

## Passion Is Vital

As you listen to each candidate describe various positions and projects, look for indications of a high level of passion regarding any areas of work. Although most applicants will have had responsibility for multiple tasks, which ones really sparked their interest? Watch for signs of enthusiasm such as increased gesturing, leaning forward, stronger voice, increased energy level, etc.

The best candidate will be the one that truly loves the responsibilities, tasks and interactions the job requires. The best candidate will be the one who has enthusiastically dealt with similar issues in the past and looks forward to tackling the problems that must be solved. The best candidate will be the one who believes the stumbling blocks that inhibit your organization's success are really stepping stones in disguise.

Too often, interviewers fail to sufficiently explore an applicant's background to uncover these areas of passion. The assumption is: if he did it in the past, he will be able to do it for us. What you seek is an individual who relishes the opportunity to initiate the projects, solve the problems or create the changes required.

The outstanding candidate will be the one who flourishes in your unique environment, who overcomes the challenges and implements the changes that will transform your organization. As you explore a candidate's past, focus on the experiences that bring out that person's passions. If the passion doesn't match the position, success is improbable.

## Fitting In

If you think about all of the employees you have hired who subsequently failed, the root cause was probably an inability to fit into your culture. Your culture is unique. Success within your organization requires compatibility with your values and style. Interdependent relationships rather than independent actions are the rule, not the exception. Interviewers often overlook these vital areas.

Those inside an organization are rarely aware of the unique nature of their culture. It is a bit like being a fish in an aquarium: to those fish, that is the entire universe. There are no lakes or rivers or oceans, or even other aquariums, just their tiny rectangle of water. Well, you are just like those fish. You cannot fully appreciate just how different you are. And just like fish, you will be the last to discover your "water."

To make the proper selection decision, understanding your culture and how it differs from other organizations is vital. An outside perspective will help you appreciate the unique characteristics required to excel in your environment. When creating your list of Critical

Success Criteria, your external advisor will play a pivotal role in defining the type of person who will be quickly assimilatcd into your system of values.

For example: Is your culture cooperative or cut-throat? Are you 24/7 or nine-to-five? Are external relationships antagonistic or symbiotic? Do you want to annihilate your competitors or partner with them? Are risks approached cautiously or audaciously? Are employee suggestions lauded or ridiculed? In some organizations, harmonious discussions in a hot tub are the norm. In others, it's like swimming with piranha.

Your external consultant can help you better understand your unique culture. This outside perspective will allow you to see your organization through the eyes of an applicant. Your advisor will guide you in creating selection criteria that help you identify those who will embrace your culture.

During each interview, you must discover the values, style, energy level and commitment to work of each applicant. It is vital to uncover the applicant's attitudes regarding employee motivation, beliefs about quality, strategy in dealing with suppliers or his process for problem solving.

Understanding the applicant's past relationships with others at all levels, both inside and outside the organization, and the nature of those relationships, is crucial. As this information is revealed, it must be compared to the Critical Success Criteria that address these issues. The candidate's capacity to thrive in your culture is one of the most accurate predictors of future employment success or failure.

## Recording Information

Writing brief notes during the interview is vital, especially if the interviewer will talk with multiple candidates over several days or weeks. After multiple interviews, the backgrounds of the candidates blur together. However, you don't want to be a court stenographer, recording every word. That would prevent you from really listening.

Although a blank notepad can be used, the best way to record information is to list the Critical Success Criteria, leaving sufficient space between items for notes. Using the Criteria list has several advantages. First, you can make very brief notes beside the appropriate criteria, tying comments to that criteria. Second, making notes by the criteria constantly reminds you of the issues you want to keep in focus, and may prompt you to ask an appropriate follow-up question to ensure understanding. By using the position criteria for notes, you will be reminded to cover each item thoroughly. Any blank spaces under one or more criteria will prompt you to continue the interview until you have gathered the necessary information.

During the interview, ask the candidate to pause if you need to write detailed notes. Most applicants will be impressed by your professionalism in recording key data and will be pleased that their responses deserved notation. What won't be clear to the candidate is: was the response positively or negatively related to your criteria? Your notes must contain all of the key facts and relevant experiences that were revealed during the interview, as this information will be shared with the other interviewers during the evaluation process.

## The Past Predicts the Future – Look for Patterns

As the applicant answers your questions, look for patterns in the responses. When discussing former bosses, are they often described as difficult people? If so, you will soon be viewed as difficult if you hire this person. Although we like to believe that we can and do change, many – if not most – personality and relationship patterns remain relatively constant throughout our lives. If someone preferred to engage in primarily solitary activities as a youth, that preference generally influences adult behavior. The risk-averse teen is rarely the thrill-seeking adult.

When listening to responses, look for patterns in such areas as task preferences, relations with coworkers, attitudes toward long work hours or extensive travel, conflict resolution strategies, meeting deadlines, negotiations with vendors or any other factors related to the Critical Success Criteria. Those past tasks and challenges that arouse a candidate's passion will be the same ones he embraces in your organization. Those issues disliked in the past will be the ones avoided in the future.

Relationships with others are almost always vital to job success. Interdependency is the norm. Probe to understand the nature of past attitudes and behaviors toward subordinates, peers, supervisors, customers, government agencies or any other critical relationships. The nature of these past relationships will generally predict the nature of future relationships within and outside your organization. If the applicant repeatedly brags about hammering suppliers into submission, you should assume that your suppliers will feel those same punishing blows. Whether that is what you want depends upon your Criteria.

## Compensation

One interviewer, usually the direct supervisor, should discuss the dreaded compensation question. Many interviewers avoid this difficult subject, but it is an essential part of the interview process. After discussing the candidate's most recent position, ask him to describe his compensation package. This would include his base salary plus any bonus, company vehicle, stock options, personal expense account, etc. If a bonus was part of the package, ask for a complete explanation of how it was determined, how much it varied from year to year, and any guaranteed minimum or absolute maximum payments.

Next, ask the candidate about future compensation expectations in terms of base, bonus or any other anticipated financial rewards. Many applicants will attempt to avoid this direct question by indicating flexibility on pay, hoping you will accept this as their answer. *That is not acceptable*. If an applicant doesn't want to provide a specific number, ask for the range of pay expected, both in salary and bonus, plus any other compensation and/or benefits expectations.

The candidate's compensation requirements should be near his present compensation. If it is dramatically higher or lower, probe to understand the discrepancy. You must establish the candidate's total compensation and benefits requirements. This is a critical part of your decision process.

However, never reject an applicant just because his compensation requirements are a bit beyond what you had hoped to pay. It is possible that once you have interviewed multiple applicants, you will find that your pay package is not consistent with the market for the level of person you hope to hire. Also, most candidates are somewhat flexible on the pay question and may be willing to accept a package that provides a bonus payment only if certain performance measures are met or exceeded. Be open to the candidate's suggestions regarding compensation and benefits options.

## Concluding the Interview

The last interviewer should conclude the interview by explaining the status and timing of the interview process. This might include the number of candidates still to be interviewed, when the initial interviews should be completed and when you hope to decide on the finalists. This final interviewer should also describe the position and answer any questions the applicant may have about the opening, the organization or any other areas of interest.

This is an excellent opportunity to describe the advantages of working for your organization. Advantages might include growth potential, financial strength, career opportunities, anticipated new products or services, technical superiority or customer satisfaction. Since you have gained a thorough understanding of the applicant's job preferences during the interview, make certain that you emphasize those aspects of the job or company that are in alignment with those needs.

If a second interview may be scheduled, tell the applicant when that decision will be made, always supplying a date weeks beyond the anticipated date. Invariably, something delays the interview or decision process, so allow plenty of time before being obligated to contact the applicant. If the candidate is indeed asked to return for a second interview, that is an easy call.

However, you also need to contact those who have been rejected. A letter or phone call to the rejected applicants should convey your appreciation for their time and interest in working for your company. Simply explain that, although they possess many talents, you have found a candidate who better matches your requirements.

If you contact rejected candidates by phone, avoid mentioning any negative aspects of their background or their shortcomings, or you will spend needless time justifying your decision. You never want to burn any bridges with rejected applicants, since it is possible that you might consider them for another position in the future.

Even if you are unable to make a decision by the date you promised, contact prospective candidates, explain the delay, and provide a new date that you are certain you can meet. Delays in the decision process will often result in the loss of a top candidate, since these individuals almost always have multiple job offers. *Keep the process on a tight schedule if you want the opportunity to select your first choice.*

# STEP FIVE

# EVALUATION AND SECOND INTERVIEWS

## Evaluation

I f possible, schedule all of the initial interviews as close together as feasible; within the same week is best. At the conclusion of the first round of interviews, all of the interviewers should meet to compare the candidates. The Critical Success Criteria are the basis for the discussion. All interviewers need to bring their notes from the interviews.

Each candidate is then compared to the Critical Success Criteria, with interviewers supporting their conclusions based on the information they gained during the interview process. Keeping the focus on the criteria and the facts that support the assessment of each interviewer ensures a more objective evaluation of an applicant's strengths and limitations.

One person should be tasked with recording the conclusions of each interviewer in relation to each of the criteria. Generally, a consensus is reached regarding how well a candidate matches the position requirements. If the interviewers disagree, the discussion should stay focused on what the applicant actually *said* during the interview, not the speculation or gut instincts of the interviewer. By keeping the discussion objective, personal bias is minimized.

## Second Interviews

After evaluating all of the applicants, you will generally agree that one or two interviewees appear to stand out from the rest in terms of your selection criteria. Before making the final choice, a second interview is invaluable. At the conclusion of the evaluation discussion, interviewers may have different opinions regarding how well a candidate matches one or more of the Critical Success Criteria. Other questions or issues may need to be clarified. A second interview allows you to address these issues in detail, plus resolve any concerns that the applicant may have.

During the second interview, you may want to further evaluate each finalist by providing a real-life problem for the applicant to consider. This problem could be a current issue that requires resolution or a significant past problem that you can describe in detail. It is often best to have your entire management team present during this problem-solving exercise so that the applicant can ask the most knowledgeable person for any required details.

In fact, the quality of the questions asked by the applicant and the level of detail requested may confirm the applicant's grasp of technical or financial aspects of this type of problem. Since the applicant will be asked for a proposed process to create a solution, you can evaluate how he would involve others – such as employees, suppliers or customers – in creating the proposed solution.

Always use real rather than fictional problems, since real problems are always more complicated and difficult than anything you could possibly make up. In addition, you can provide real facts and numbers as well as any limitations on proposed solutions. Rather than expecting a brilliant resolution to your problem, evaluate the candidate's questions, suggested process, assumptions of time required, involvement of others, self-imposed limitations, funding requirements and staffing suggestions.

At the end of your discussion, you should have a much clearer picture of the technical knowledge, financial understanding, management style and general approach that this applicant will exhibit if hired. As the candidate describes his approach, process or solution, ask probing follow-up questions to ensure your understanding. Of course, compare the applicant's response to the Critical Success Criteria to ensure that you have a good match. Any apparent mismatches should be discussed as a group after the applicant has left the meeting.

At the conclusion of the second interview, a group lunch or dinner is recommended. It allows the candidate an opportunity to observe the group dynamics and get to know the individuals that he will be working with on a more personal level.

Remember, top candidates generally have multiple job opportunities, so they will be evaluating your organization and management team relative to other potential offers. During a relaxing meal, the candidate will have the opportunity to ask questions and resolve issues while you describe the innumerable benefits of working for your company.

# STEP SIX

# BACKGROUND CHECK AND JOB OFFER

## Background Investigation

Your selection process isn't complete until you have conducted a background check. This investigation not only confirms the facts, such as dates of employment, positions held, education and other relevant information. It should also confirm that the applicant matches the Critical Success Criteria.

The most effective method for obtaining a comprehensive evaluation of the potential new hire is to talk with direct supervisors, suppliers, customers, subordinates or others who have worked with the candidate. Consider employing the services of a firm that specializes in conducting background checks to investigate such areas as education, licensing, dates of employment, criminal convictions and credit history.

During the initial interview, you should have asked for the names and phone numbers of people who have intimate knowledge of the applicant's employment background. If the applicant is currently employed, ask for the names of anyone inside or outside the company who could confidentially confirm basic employment information and evaluate the candidate's abilities. For previous employers, the direct supervisor is generally the best source of information. Even if that supervisor is no longer with the former employer, the candidate can often obtain a current phone number.

*Make those calls!* They take only ten to fifteen minutes each and will provide you with a more complete picture of the candidate. Using the Critical Success Criteria, ask open-ended questions about job duties, budget responsibilities, accomplishments, management style, peer relations, shortcomings or any important factors. Ask how the individual could have been more effective, and inquire as to the type of environment that best suits your candidate. *Never reveal your criteria or suggest a possible answer.* Remember: there are no wrong answers, only honest answers. Record all of the information provided and note any inconsistencies or possible areas of concern.

**Final Choice and Job Offer**

By now, one candidate should have risen to the top of your list. If possible, meet with this person to make the job offer. If that is not practical, a phone offer can be nearly as effective. You already know the compensation that the candidate wants or requires and you know what you would like to pay. If those numbers match, the monetary offer is simple. If not, propose a compensation package, but allow room for negotiations on such issues as relocation expense reimbursement, a one-time bonus based on completing a specific project or a signing bonus. If this person has a proven track record and a management style that are consistent with your Critical Success Criteria, some flexibility on compensation is warranted.

Be receptive to other needs of your finalist. Often, candidates may be willing to accept less pay in exchange for something else of value. Something as simple as a different job title can hold significant value for some people. Keep an open mind regarding the needs of the candidate as you finalize the offer.

During this offer discussion, emphasize all of the benefits of working for your company. Since during the interview you learned what motivates this person, emphasize all the aspects of the job and organization that are consistent with the candidate's preferences. Consult your interview notes to recall those factors that are important to the candidate and describe how your organization can fulfill those needs. You must sell top candidates on your organization, as these individuals almost always have several job opportunities to consider.

After all of the details of your hiring offer have been finalized, write your new hire a letter confirming every item. Many employment deals have disintegrated when the memory of the hiring manager didn't match the memory of the new employee. In the letter, ask the person to review everything listed to ensure agreement. For any issues in question, make certain that you discuss and resolve the disputes, writing a second letter if appropriate.

In your offer letter, make the tone warm and personal. Emphasize the characteristics of your organization that are consistent with the individual's needs and desires that were uncovered during the interview. Remember that you need to sell such a highly-qualified candidate on the benefits of working for your company.

## Disclose Any Negative Information

Before finalizing the deal, make sure that you have disclosed any negative information about your organization that might influence a candidate's decision to accept the position. Make sure that you mention minor details such as the impending bankruptcy of the business, the indictment of your CEO, the threatened delisting of your stock, the loss of a major client or any other relevant information.

## Establish Performance Measures

If you haven't done so already, explain in detail your expectations in terms of job performance. Describe projects that must be completed, problems that require immediate attention, relationships inside or outside the organization that must be improved, financial issues that must be resolved or other expectations regarding performance.

First, describe the issues that require immediate attention and resolution within three to twelve months. Discuss each problem in intricate detail, answering any questions that the candidate may have. *Hold nothing back.* This is the time for full disclosure. Be brutally honest in describing the measures for success, critical deadlines, financial limitations, penalties for failure or any other potential negative factors. If you scare him off with your honest description of the job challenges, it is better now than a month after he has accepted the position.

Next, provide an outline of your longer-term goals and expectations. Describe in as much detail as possible where you expect the candidate's department or division to be in one to three years. Include sales levels, profit goals, project implementations, quality measures, customer satisfaction, supplier issues or other measures of success. Again, encourage questions and provide complete answers, including any possible impediments to achieving these goals.

To make certain that you have communicated effectively, ask *the candidate* to provide a written summary of this discussion. This will ensure that you have provided a clear description of your goals for the position and the measures of success. It will help clarify your expectations in the mind of the candidate, and provide him with a comprehensive list of the tasks that require attention. Should the candidate's summary contain any inaccuracies, it will allow you to clarify any issues in dispute.

# THE PROCESS WORKS FOR ANY POSITION

## Applying the Process to Other Jobs

Up until now, this book has described a hiring process for senior positions. A similar process is just as effective for any position in your organization, including entry-level jobs. In some ways, this process works better for junior-level or entry-level positions, since you have more information available due to the high volume of successes and failures.

For example, if you apply the process to an entry-level factory position or retail clerk, you have multiple examples of both those employees who have excelled and those who were quickly terminated. All of these data can be mined to look for patterns of success and failure.

First, interview those employees who are your top performers in this position. Look for anything they have in common, such as prior work experience or education. Attempt to uncover common values, attitudes or behaviors that appear to predict success. In addition, talk with others who have direct knowledge of the position regarding the factors that predict success.

Using input from this top-performing group, their direct supervisors and others who understand the position, create a list of Critical Success Criteria for this job. Consider any physical requirements, the need to work outside or in a harsh environment, customer contact, the ability to handle money, phone skills, technical or product knowledge, work stress or hours of work. Ask the top performers what they believe is essential for success. Ask them to provide examples of former employees who failed, and why those individuals were unwilling or unable to perform.

If possible, interview employees who failed in this position. Sometimes these individuals have transferred to other positions, but often they have left the organization. Their insight can prove invaluable. Consider asking your external consultant to gather this information.

Why use an external advisor to contact these former workers? First, many individuals who quit are often reluctant to criticize a former employer. That employer could retaliate by providing a negative reference to prospective employers. Second, for those who were fired, gaining their cooperation is more likely if the person calling is not directly associated with the former employer.

The information gained from former employees provides a unique perspective regarding both the position and the organization. In talking with them, you may learn of safety concerns, inter-departmental conflicts, abusive supervisors or other negative factors. You may discover that your pay levels are not competitive, the work scheduling is unfair, the training is inadequate or the hiring supervisor selects employees due to their bountiful cleavage. Although fired employees may be motivated by vengeance, they often provide you with meaningful information that helps explain your employee turnover. If several former employees voice the same concern, you should at least investigate their claims before dismissing it as false.

Former employees will help you discover shortcomings in your hiring process, since they failed for some identifiable reason. Perhaps the job was not clearly described or the arduous working conditions were not fully disclosed. Perhaps the skills, abilities and personality traits required for success are not understood by those making the hiring decisions. At the conclusion of these interviews, you will have a better understanding of your selection deficiencies and the steps required to reduce these errors in the future.

Just as with senior positions, the best interview process starts by involving all the interviewers in a planning meeting. Consider including coworkers or other non-traditional individuals in the selection process, especially those with a strong understanding of the position.

Using the process described previously, create a list of duties, tasks, educational needs, technical requirements, prior work experience, certifications and other relevant information. As before, spend considerable time discussing the type of person who best fits the position and who will most likely succeed in your work environment and culture.

At the conclusion of your meeting, you should have created the Critical Success Criteria for this position and have reached agreement on how these criteria will be defined, measured or evaluated. The actual interview process and final evaluation processes are the same as for senior-level jobs, although the interviews themselves are generally shorter in duration.

Unlike senior-level positions, the Critical Success Criteria for lower-level jobs can be employed frequently since the volume of hiring is much greater. Also, over time, you can modify both the selection process and the criteria based on the performance of multiple new employees, improving your ratio of successful hires. Although the time to initially create the Critical Success Criteria may seem excessive for entry-level positions, the cost is insignificant when spread over multiple hires. This is especially true when the significant costs associated with employee turnover are considered.

## Work Simulations

One of the best methods for evaluating entry- to mid-level positions is to create a work simulation. This simulation should be as close to the actual job as possible, be designed to quickly sort the better performers from the rest of the applicants and include objective measures of success. The simulation should generally take less than an hour to complete.

For example, a job that requires using specific software knowledge can be simulated by asking each applicant to complete a task or solve a problem using that software. If possible, design the simulation to evaluate the level of knowledge from a basic understanding through advanced competency.

Other simulations could include assembly tasks to measure manual dexterity, word processing projects that include both easy and difficult requirements, accounting entries at various levels of complexity or computer or manual drafting assignments. In each case, make the simulation as real as possible, including time deadlines that are difficult but achievable. Ask employees who actually perform the job duties to assist you in designing a realistic simulation, including the methods for evaluating performance on a sliding scale from "very poor" to "excellent."

In some cases, you may be able to use one or more actual job tasks to evaluate prospective employees. There are two advantages to using the actual job. First, you can directly measure applicants' abilities to perform the task or tasks. Second, applicants will experience the real job duties, allowing them to decide if the job meets their expectations.

In addition, applicants will be exposed to the work environment, which could be dirty or noisy or crowded or involve some other factors that could influence their decision to accept the job. Even if you can't allow the applicants to perform the actual job tasks, you may want to show them the work environment if that appears to be a cause of employee turnover.

Regardless of the work simulation you create, it will almost always produce a more successful new hire than doing nothing to evaluate potential applicants. Not only have you had the opportunity to observe and measure a candidate in a real work situation, the applicant has also had the chance to experience the job before accepting your offer. The cost of developing a simulation is quickly recovered by reducing your cost of turnover.

# A SIMPLE BUT EFFECTIVE PROCESS

Effective interviews are much more than an unstructured conversation related to vague thoughts regarding position requirements. Effective interviews involve much more than a casual discussion followed by a delusional decision based solely on gut feelings. Effective interviews go way beyond the unprofessional approach where the interviewer talks more than the interviewee, learning little while divulging carelessly conceived criteria.

To select top-notch talent, you must invest the time to understand the requirements of the position and the culture of your organization. This knowledge will help you create the Critical Success Criteria that will guide the entire selection process, allowing you to ask the laser-accurate questions that separate the outstanding candidates from the less qualified. The result: an infusion of excellent employees that will propel your organization to outstanding levels of performance.

# APPENDIX A

# SAMPLE QUESTIONS

The following questions will help you obtain the information you require during the employment interview. Use them as they are written or modify them in any way that suits your needs. In most cases, the questions are open-ended, encouraging a lengthy and complete response. Remember: gaining information regarding the candidate's abilities, knowledge, attitudes or preferences in relation to the Critical Success Criteria guides every question you ask.

## EDUCATION

Why did you choose (college/university)?
What was your major and why did you choose that field of study?
What were your career goals or expectations at that time?
Which courses did you enjoy most? Why?
Which courses did you like least? Why?
If you were to start school over, what would you do differently?
What activities were you involved in while you were in school?
What did you learn from these activities? How did they help you grow as a person?
Why did you fail to graduate?
Why did you change majors?
In thinking of your major, how have you applied that knowledge to your work?
How did school change your views, outlook, values or attitudes?
What have you done since school to stay current in your profession?

## WORK EXPERIENCE

What was your first relevant job?

Why did you choose that company/organization?

Describe your initial position in detail. How long were you in that job?

What was your next position? Describe your duties and responsibilities.

What did you like most about that job? Least?

What did you learn from that position?

What was your biggest accomplishment?

What was your biggest disappointment?

What was your budget? What was your role in creating and monitoring that budget?

Did you have any employees reporting to you? How many? What were their duties?

Who were your peers? What were their positions and responsibilities? Describe your relationship with these peers.

Who was your direct supervisor? What was his or her job title and duties? Can you provide a current phone number for this person? Describe your relationship with this supervisor.

Was there anyone else inside the organization with whom you had regular contact? Please explain the nature of these relationships.

Was there anyone outside the organization with whom you had contact? Please describe the nature of these relationships.

What did you learn from working for this company?

Why did you leave this organization?

Describe in detail your favorite: boss; peer; subordinate; job task; work environment; relationship outside the organization.

Describe in detail your least favorite: boss; peer; subordinate; job task; work environment; relationship outside the organization.

Describe an ideal: job; boss; employees; work environment.

## SELF-ASSESSMENT

What are your career goals in the short term? Long term?

What are your greatest strengths? Weaknesses?

What would make you more effective?

What is your management style?

How do you motivate employees? Please provide several examples.

How do you deal with employee performance failures? Please provide a few examples.

Describe your relationships with peers, both positive and negative.

How do you manage those above you in the organization?

What type of boss is best for you?

What have you done to improve your technical or management skills?

What type of work environment do you prefer?

What sort of compensation system best motivates you (e.g., bonus based on performance; straight salary; commission; ownership; stock options)?

What haven't you shared with me about your prior work experiences, relationships, accomplishments or yourself that you feel I should know?

## OTHER-ASSESSMENT

If I put all of your employees at (company) together in a room and asked them to describe you as a boss, what would they say? What would they say are your best traits? How would they describe your management style? How would they describe your approach to discipline? What would they suggest you could do to be more effective?

If I put all of your peers at (company) in a room and asked them to describe you, what would they say? What would they say are your best traits? How would they describe your management style? How would they describe your relationship with them? What would they suggest you could do to be more effective?

When I call (your direct supervisor), how will he describe you? What will he say are your strengths? Weaknesses? What will he say were your biggest accomplishments? In what areas will he say your performance fell below expectations? What changes will he say you could or did make to improve your effectiveness?

How would customers, suppliers, government agencies, etc., describe you?

## NEXT JOB

What is a logical next position for you? Please describe.

What is your salary, bonus and other compensation at your current job?

If you received a bonus, how was it determined? What was the minimum and maximum? What was your bonus for each year or period?

What are your expectations for compensation in your next position?

Although no one has a perfect job, including us, describe an ideal next job. Include duties, employees, supervisor, peers, organization and anything else that is important.

What kind of projects, challenges, problems or initiatives would you want as part of an ideal job?

Considering all of the jobs you have held, what do you want to avoid or minimize in your next job?

## PROBING QUESTIONS

Oh?

How much/many?

Please provide the: dollars; numbers; percentages; other hard data.

Could you be more specific?

What was the result?

How could you have improved the outcome?

What would you do differently next time?

Who else was involved? What were their responsibilities?

Tell me more.

Please give me an example.

What caused it to fail?

Who was responsible?

Why did that happen?

What would have produced a better result or outcome?

What did you learn from that experience?

How did your boss react? Peers? Employees? Customers? Suppliers?

How did you feel about that?

How did you apply this knowledge to future projects?

Oh?

# APPENDIX B

# HIRING PROCESS CHECKLIST

This book contains a vast amount of information that may be difficult to recall. Below is a brief listing of each major step in the process. Use this list as a reminder of the actions you wish to take.

## Step One – Establish Your Selection Criteria

Analyze your organization, including products, services, new offerings and the role of the new hire in all of these areas.

- List all the people inside and outside the organization that the individual will interact with and the nature of those interactions.
- Review the job description for technical skills, knowledge, education, certification or similar requirements.
- List the routine, day-to-day tasks and duties of the position.
- List critical problems, crucial projects, or pivotal relations that must be addressed by the new hire.
- List the type and level of prior work experience needed.
- Talk with supervisors, peers, subordinates or others who can provide insight into the requirements of the position.
- Find an outside advisor to assist you in seeing your organization with fresh eyes, especially your culture and values.
- Interview employees, both management and non-management, regarding their knowledge of the position and the nature of their relationship to the position.
- Interview customers, suppliers, vendors and government agencies with whom the new hire must interact to gain their perspective on the position's requirements.
- Invite three to five managers/staff plus your external advisor to assist you in developing the Critical Success Criteria.

- As a group, list the skills, abilities, knowledge, education, certification and so forth required for success.
- Next, list the prior work experience that is essential, including the specific tasks, duties and responsibilities.
- List the important projects, critical problems, relationship issues, etc., that the new hire must tackle.
- Consider any special requirements, such as extensive travel, weekend work, 24/7 operations, etc.
- Define your culture by listing words or phrases that describe your business philosophies, approach to customers or attitude regarding quality.
- List the personality characteristics, style, work ethic or values that a potential new hire must possess.
- Refine your list to the most crucial four to five skills, three to five work experiences, three to five personality characteristics and any unique requirements, such as travel.
- Decide on the essential six to nine Critical Success Criteria and clearly define the meaning of each.

## Step Two – Start Your Search

- Interview any current employees that are a close match to the Critical Success Criteria.
- Interview these internal candidates just as you would an outsider.
- If no internal employees meet your requirements, advertise your opening, ask for referrals and/or hire a search firm to find suitable candidates.

## Step Three – Prepare for the Interview

- Develop an interview strategy, including the sequence you plan to follow.
- Review each resume and note any specific questions you have for that candidate.

## Step Four – Conduct the Interview

- Clear your schedule to allow at least two hours for the interview.
- If possible, find a conference room or other site away from your office to conduct the interview.
- Meet the applicant and describe the outline or sequence you plan to follow.

- Start the interview by asking about education or the first relevant position.
- Encourage the candidate to provide details on the nature and level of responsibilities of each position.
- Explore relationships with peers, subordinates and superiors.
- Ask for the phone numbers of several prior supervisors.
- Discuss relationships with others by asking how those individuals would describe the candidate.
- Remember: there are no wrong answers, only honest answers; avoid telegraphing any negative feedback regarding any answer.
- Listening is more than hearing – avoid telling any favorite stories.
- Periodically paraphrase what you have learned to ensure understanding.
- Ask the tough questions, then shut up!
- Remember that silence is your friend.
- Use probing questions to keep the candidate talking about areas of interest to you.
- Look for the applicant's passion regarding any aspect of your Critical Success Criteria.
- Ask questions to ensure that the interviewee will fit your unique culture and shares common values.
- Record brief notes during the interview that are relevant to your criteria.
- Since the past predicts the future, look for patterns in terms of past relationships, job interests and so on.
- Discuss the compensation requirements of the candidate.
- Conclude the interview by explaining the timing of the interview process and when second interviews will be scheduled.

## Step Five – Evaluation and Second Interviews
- Meet with all of the interviewers to compare the candidates.
- Evaluate candidates based on information they provided compared to the Critical Success Criteria.
- Schedule second interviews with the top one or two applicants.
- Address any questions, discrepancies in opinion or other unresolved issues.
- Provide a real-life problem for the candidate to address.

- Evaluate the candidate's questions and suggested process rather than seeking brilliant, immediate solutions to your problem.
- Consider a group lunch or dinner as a way to create a relaxed environment for the candidate to get acquainted with your management team.

## Step Six – Background Check and Offer

- Contact as many previous direct supervisors as practical; ask questions to confirm or deny the person's work experience, management style and preferred environment compared to the Critical Success Criteria.
- Hire a background checking firm to verify the education, licensing, dates of employment, criminal convictions, credit history, etc.
- Make the job offer in person, if possible.
- Describe the position, compensation package and advantages of working for your organization.
- Put the offer in writing to ensure that an agreement has been reached.
- During this meeting, disclose any negative information about the company that might affect the candidate's decision to accept the offer.
- Describe in detail your expectations in terms of issues that require attention, projects that must be completed, relationships that must be improved, etc.
- Provide your longer-term goals for the position and measures of success.
- Ask the candidate to write a letter summarizing all the short-term and long-term job requirements described above.

## The Process Works for Any Position

- Consider other positions that would benefit from an improved selection process.
- Interview the top performers in each position to gain insight into the work requirements.
- Interview direct supervisors and others who have specific knowledge of the targeted position.
- Contact current or former employees who failed to perform

in this job (or quit) to understand any underlying problems or issues that are causing turnover.

- Select interviewers and meet to create the Critical Success Criteria for this position.
- Develop a work simulation that mirrors the requirements of the position in every way possible, including work environment.
- Create an objective scoring system for the simulation.

# ABOUT THE AUTHOR

Steve Springer has over thirty years of experience as a seasoned executive and Human Resources professional. He has personally interviewed thousands of people and hired many hundreds of employees at all levels, from entry level to senior executives earning over $1 million per year. His vast knowledge of the hiring process gained through three decades of experience has been distilled into this effective how-to book on employee selection.

Majoring in Human Resources, Steve earned a BS-Business Administration degree from The Ohio State University in 1972. His early HR career involved hiring entry- and mid-level employees. It was then that he first developed a selection process which separated future successes from future failures. In later positions, he further honed his recruiting skills as he hired a broad range of employees, with emphasis on professionals and middle managers.

In 1983, Pulte Homes sought Steve's skills. Starting as Director-HR, he soon advanced to Vice President-HR, with full responsibility for all aspects of human resources for the entire corporation. One of Steve's primary tasks was recruiting top talent for Pulte's corporate office and field operations. This required a comprehensive understanding of the skills, abilities and personality that were vital for success in Pulte's unique culture.

Steve also identified an excessive employee turnover problem that was hindering growth. Knowing the bottom-line impact of reduced turnover, Steve immediately created an employee selection training process that played a vital role in dramatically reducing the loss of employee talent.

Steve has taken the knowledge gained from his thousands of interviews and his powerful training course and condensed it into a single book. His goal: provide the readers with a simple but effective process that will consistently deliver outstanding employees.